The Coastal Birder's
Journal

Notes

A loon can dive as deep as sixty metres.

May

The Victoria Day weekend is often time for another twenty-four-hour Big Day for British Columbia birders who identify many species by sound rather than sight. They begin at midnight or 2 a.m. by listening for owls. As twilight approaches, the dawn chorus brings the songs of flycatchers, warblers, and other upland species. Many coastal birders travel to the interior in May for the Okanagan Big Day Challenge, held to raise money for habitat protection.

The earliest chicks of red-breasted sapsuckers, northern flickers, and downy, hairy, and pileated woodpeckers begin to curiously peer out from their nesting cavities. These birds will nest in boxes but prefer holes in natural snags. You can create a snag from a piece of alder, maple, or birch about three or five metres long. Lay it on moist ground and cover it with leaves in the fall: within two years the wood should be suitably soft and the snag can be erected.

California quail with their offspring are conspicuous in May near nesting sites on southern Vancouver Island and in the Fraser delta. They are most abundant between Victoria and Saanich Peninsula. Look for them in shrublands dominated by blackberry and broom, on powerline rights-of-way and golf courses, and in parks and gardens. These endearing birds were introduced to Victoria and the Fraser delta in the late 1800s, then to the Queen Charlottes and South Pender Island around 1910.

Observation Records

DATE	LOCATION	SPECIES	NO.	REMARKS

Observation Records

DATE	LOCATION	SPECIES	NO.	REMARKS

Observation Records

DATE	LOCATION	SPECIES	NO.	REMARKS

Flickers feed on the ground more than any other woodpecker.

It was once thought that swallows hibernated in the muddy bottoms of streams and lakes.

Notes

A nuthatch always moves headfirst down a tree trunk.

June

Some backyard birders confine their early summer observations to their own homes. For people who raise swallows, wrens, chickadees, sparrows, starlings, or other species in artificial nest boxes, June is a good month to watch the constant flutter of adults coming and going with food for the young. Eventually the tiny beak of the first chick pokes through the entrance hole to survey the immense world beyond the nest. Some adult pairs may raise two, even three, broods in one season.

The first ducklings and goslings begin to follow their parents as they forage in ponds, lakes, and slow-flowing streams. The only cygnets you'll likely see on the B.C. coast are mute swans, an introduced species which breeds only on southern Vancouver Island between Duncan and Sooke. Canada geese with goslings, however, are seen near freshwater nesting sites along the entire coast. Adult pairs are usually accompanied by about half a dozen offspring. The ubiquitous mallard, with strings of five, eight, even twenty ducklings trailing behind, shares marshy nesting habitats with Canada geese. Other coastal waterfowl with offspring in June include wood ducks, teals, pintails, wigeon, harlequins, and mergansers.

June is also a good month to practise bird-song identification. Of particular interest are nighthawks, white-crowned sparrows, Swainson's thrushes, and screeching juvenile great horned owls following adults.

Observation Records

DATE	LOCATION	SPECIES	NO.	REMARKS

Observation Records

DATE	LOCATION	SPECIES	NO.	REMARKS

Observation Records

DATE	LOCATION	SPECIES	NO.	REMARKS

A newly hatched robin weighing seven grams may eat up to fourteen worms a day.

A male house wren sings its courtship song about six thousand times a day.

Notes

A male wren builds up to six nests and the female chooses the one she likes best.

July

Though officially midsummer, July marks the start of southbound autumn migrations for many coastal shorebirds. It's a particularly dramatic time, with flocks numbering in the thousands. There are least, spotted, and western sandpipers, short-billed dowitchers, black-bellied and semipalmated plovers, killdeer, yellowlegs, whimbrels, curlews, godwits, sanderlings, and more. This impressive exodus continues into September, providing excellent summer birding on tidal flats and salt marshes. There's outstanding shorebird watching at Sidney Spit Provincial Park, Parksville, Qualicum, Kye Bay near Comox, Long Beach and Tofino, Brooks Peninsula, Cape Scott, Boundary Bay, Hakai Recreation Area, and on the Queen Charlottes at Naikoon Provincial Park, Sandspit, and Masset Inlet.

The most abundant bird on rockier shores at this time is the black turnstone, which gathers in flocks of four thousand on the north coast, or about two thousand on the east coast of Vancouver Island. The turnstone shares its shores with the black oystercatcher, a crow-sized shorebird with a bright orange beak and yellow eyes ringed in orange. The end of the oystercatcher's bill is vertically flat, a tool to insert into mussels and other bivalves and sever the adductor muscle, forcing the shells apart.

California gulls are moving south in July, and Heermann's gulls, which breed in the Gulf of California, appear in B.C. in late July and August, still wearing their bright summer plumage.

Observation Records

DATE	LOCATION	SPECIES	NO.	REMARKS

Observation Records

DATE	LOCATION	SPECIES	NO.	REMARKS

Observation Records

DATE	LOCATION	SPECIES	NO.	REMARKS

At least six million seabirds breed on the Pacific Northwest coast.

The Alaska oil spill of 1989 killed nearly six hundred thousand seabirds.

Notes

It is estimated that a Clark's nutcracker can store approximately thirty thousand pine seeds in a single season.

August

The tiny Bonaparte's gull, with its distinctive black hood, emits a high-pitched screech as it swarms over turbulent tide rips, diving for small baitfish. Nicknamed the "coho gull," this adept fisher is often seen by sport fishermen in August when coho salmon feed on the baitfish. Bonaparte's flocks are enormous at this time of year—up to twenty-five thousand near Comox, ten thousand at Discovery Passage near Campbell River. Flocks of one and two thousand are common.

This agile bird is relentlessly stalked by the parasitic jaeger, a long-tailed piratical gull that flies like a falcon, harassing the Bonaparte's gull until it disgorges its prey.

Great blue herons, now finished nesting, are conspicuous in late summer. As tall as a six-year-old child, they stand in the shallows on their spindly, knobby-kneed legs, long necks hunched into their shoulders, waiting for unwary fish to pass. Groups of one hundred to three hundred feed at this time on the mud flats at Boundary Bay, Crescent Beach, and Roberts Bank. Gatherings of three and four dozen are found at Sidney Spit Provincial Park, site of the largest heronry in the Gulf Islands. Recent studies in Georgia Strait show that great blue herons, the most abundant and widely distributed of B.C.'s six heron species, are being adversely affected by dioxins and furans, which damage embryos.

Observation Records

DATE	LOCATION	SPECIES	NO.	REMARKS

Observation Records

DATE	LOCATION	SPECIES	NO.	REMARKS

Observation Records

DATE	LOCATION	SPECIES	NO.	REMARKS

Cormorants, which take to the air into the wind, invariably nest on the windward side of islands.

British Columbia's nine alcid species comprise 80 percent of the province's nesting seabirds.

Notes

_____

_____

_____

_____

_____

_____

_____

_____

_____

_____

_____

_____

_____

_____

_____

_____

_____

_____

_____

_____

_____

_____

_____

_____

_____

British Columbia's 1.2 million nesting pairs of Cassin's auklets
are about four-fifths of the world's total population of the species.

September

As the last days of summer surrender to fall, many birds move out, to be gradually replaced by those that settle in for winter. In recent years birders have realized there's a significant raptor migration on southern Vancouver Island. Sharp-shinned hawks, peregrine falcons, goshawks, harriers, and others all seem to pass through in September. Groups of nearly five hundred turkey vultures, a species which appears to be increasing, congregate on the south island.

One particularly startling event is the virtual disappearance of bald eagles from the Victoria area. With their fledglings gone, the adults move toward nearby salmon-spawning streams such as the Cowichan, Nanaimo, or Qualicum, then return in a month or two.

About a million northern pintails migrate along the coast and huge flocks arrive in Georgia Strait and Puget Sound in September to set up camp for the winter. Ten thousand have appeared in one group at Port Hardy; three or four thousand may arrive at Reifel Migratory Bird Sanctuary, in the Fraser delta, along with six thousand mallards and a variety of other waterfowl and upland birds.

Many seagoing waterfowl species—harlequins, goldeneye, buffleheads, scoters, mergansers—begin to appear in large numbers along coastal shores in late September.

Observation Records

DATE	LOCATION	SPECIES	NO.	REMARKS

Observation Records

DATE	LOCATION	SPECIES	NO.	REMARKS

Observation Records

DATE	LOCATION	SPECIES	NO.	REMARKS

A three-day-old ancient murrelet can avoid predators by taking to the sea at night. By dawn it may be forty kilometres offshore and might remain at sea for two years.

The 272,000 pairs of ancient murrelets inhabiting British Columbia waters are about three-quarters of the world's total population of the species.

Notes

More than six million ducks, swans and geese migrate through the Pacific Northwest.

October

The first frosts of October are a signal to prepare winter bird feeders. If you're building new feeders, consider that wet, moldy feed is fatal to birds: a roofed feeder is best. If you prefer a tray, put out just enough seed for each day. Place the feeders near trees, shrubs, or other cover for hasty escapes from predators.

White or yellow millet is a staple in a bird's diet. Hulled sunflower seeds and crushed peanuts have a high fat content which helps warm up cold birds. Chick scratch, which doesn't sprout, is a mix of cracked wheat and corn that's enjoyed by most birds. Larger birds, such as pigeons or Steller's jays, like cracked corn, wheat, and barley. A good home-made small-bird mix is millet, hulled sunflower seeds, grain and seed chips and crushed peanuts (two parts each), and chick scratch (one part).

Suet, which can be hung in a wire mesh cage, is particularly enticing to woodpeckers, chickadees, nuthatches, and other clinging birds. A few weeks' supply consists of one kilogram of lard, three hundred millilitres of oatmeal, five hundred grams of cornmeal, and five hundred millilitres each of wild bird seed, sunflower seed, and currants. Melt the lard, mix in the ingredients and let it cool outside, stirring it occasionally to maintain a regular consistency. Then wrap feeder-sized cakes in wax paper and freeze them until they're needed.

Observation Records

DATE	LOCATION	SPECIES	NO.	REMARKS

Observation Records

DATE	LOCATION	SPECIES	NO.	REMARKS

Observation Records

DATE	LOCATION	SPECIES	NO.	REMARKS

Seventy percent of the waterfowl habitat in the Fraser delta has been alienated by residential and industrial development.

A bald eagle has approximately seventy-two hundred feathers. The feathers, about 550 grams, weigh twice as much as the bones.

Notes

Sixty or seventy percent of all ducks fall victim to predators during their first year of life.

November

A major birding attraction this month is the peak of the snow goose migration at Reifel Migratory Bird Sanctuary in the Fraser delta. The geese begin showing up in September and October, and by November forty thousand are feeding on the foreshore and adjacent fields, luring thousands of visitors to the sanctuary. The striking white plumage of these geese may be stained a rusty red from mineral deposits in the foraging areas. This goose also appears in a "blue phase," which was once considered a separate species. Both white and blue snow geese are found on this coast.

All of the snow geese migrating through the Fraser delta breed on Wrangel Island off eastern Siberia, where about 100,000 have nested in recent years. That number is down from about 400,000 in 1960: conservationists hope to help boost the breeding population to 120,000 by the turn of the century.

November is also a good month for large flocks of Canada geese; ten thousand or more gather at Tofino, four and five thousand on northern Vancouver Island, and two and three thousand at various sites on the Queen Charlotte Islands. Flocks of twenty-five thousand Bonaparte's gulls and thirty thousand mew gulls are counted off the Victoria waterfront at this time. This is also the time when wintering trumpeter swans return from their northern nesting grounds.

Observation Records

DATE	LOCATION	SPECIES	NO.	REMARKS

Observation Records

DATE	LOCATION	SPECIES	NO.	REMARKS

Observation Records

DATE	LOCATION	SPECIES	NO.	REMARKS

Two million mallards migrate on the Pacific flyway; at least forty thousand winter in the Pacific Northwest.

A mallard has approximately twelve thousand feathers. A tundra swan has approximately twenty-five thousand feathers.

Notes

As many as nine hundred thousand American wigeon migrate on the Pacific flyway and sixty thousand winter in the Fraser delta.

December

In the height of the festive season, thousands of birders across the continent don winter woollies and flock to the outdoors to count birds in nearly two thousand communities. The North American Christmas Bird Count is co-ordinated by the National Audubon Society, which sets the rules. Each community's birders must count the same area every year on a specific day during a two-week period around Christmas and New Year's. The society publishes the results: these long-term records provide information on population trends, migration patterns, periodic fluctuations, species distribution, and other important bird facts.

The idea of a Christmas Bird Count originated in 1900, when American naturalist Frank Chapman decided to change the British tradition of hunting birds on Boxing Day to counting them.

Some coastal bird count records: 44,832 glaucous-winged gulls at Ladner on December 28, 1980, an all-time North American high; 472 hooded mergansers at Victoria on December 27, 1970, an all-time Canadian high; 411 killdeer at Ladner on December 22, 1962, an all-time Canadian high.

Bald eagles are still picking at carcasses left from salmon spawns during December—counts include a thousand at Rivers Inlet on the central coast, four hundred at Deep Bay, three hundred at Harrison, and two hundred each at Comox and Squamish.

As many as seven thousand Brandt's cormorants celebrate Christmas in Active Pass and five thousand Canada geese gather at Reifel Migratory Bird Sanctuary.

Observation Records

DATE	LOCATION	SPECIES	NO.	REMARKS

Observation Records

DATE	LOCATION	SPECIES	NO.	REMARKS

Observation Records

DATE	LOCATION	SPECIES	NO.	REMARKS

Freshly hatched grebelings are carried on the back of a parent; they climb into a pocket formed by the back feathers and wings of the adult grebe.

It is estimated that birds in the United States drop one million pellets every minute.

Notes

It is estimated that in North America thirty million cats kill one hundred million birds a year.

Coastal Birding Sites

Every birder has his or her favourite local beach, lake, marsh, or wood-land. There are thousands of birding areas in B.C., many with trails, blinds, viewing towers, and interpretive centres. Some are officially designated federal or provincial sanctuaries, often maintained by non-profit societies. Here is a list of B.C.'s most popular birding sites.

Vancouver Island/Gulf Islands

1. **Active Pass:** seabirds, waterfowl, raptors
2. **Bunsby Islands:** seabirds
3. **Buttertubs Slough:** waterfowl, songbirds
4. **Cluxewe estuary:** aquatic birds, songbirds
5. **Cowichan estuary:** waterfowl, raptors
6. **Dudley Marsh:** waterfowl
7. **East Sooke Park:** autumn raptor migration
8. **Englishman estuary:** waterfowl, raptors
9. **Esquimalt Lagoon:** waterfowl, seabirds, shorebirds
10. **Fulford Harbour:** waterfowl, shorebirds, swans, eagles
11. **Island View Beach:** seabirds, raptors, songbirds
12. **Lazo Marsh:** waterfowl, raptors
13. **Martindale Flats:** waterfowl, trumpeter swans, raptors
14. **Mittlenatch Island:** nesting seabirds
15. **Nanaimo estuary:** waterfowl, raptors
16. **Nanoose:** migratory birds resting
17. **Northumberland Channel:** seabirds, eagles
18. **Pacific Rim National Park:** seabirds, shorebirds, raptors, songbirds
19. **Parksville/Qualicum:** waterfowl, brant, shorebirds
20. **Puntledge estuary:** waterfowl, shorebirds
21. **Rosewall Creek:** waterfowl, shorebirds
22. **Sidney Spit:** aquatic birds, herons, eagles, songbirds
23. **Somenos Lake:** waterfowl
24. **Swan Lake/Christmas Hill:** waterfowl, songbirds
25. **Tsehum Harbour:** seabirds, herons, eagles
26. **Victoria Harbour:** seabirds, waterfowl

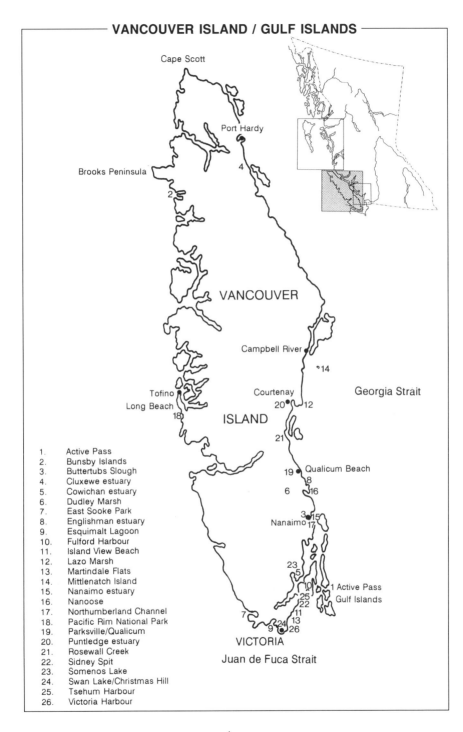

VANCOUVER ISLAND / GULF ISLANDS

Cape Scott

Port Hardy

4

Brooks Peninsula

2

VANCOUVER

Campbell River

°14

Tofino

Courtenay

Georgia Strait

Long Beach

20 12

18

ISLAND

21

19 Qualicum Beach

8

6 16

3 15

Nanaimo 17

23

5

10 1 Active Pass

25 Gulf Islands

22

7 11

24 13

9 26

VICTORIA

Juan de Fuca Strait

1. Active Pass
2. Bunsby Islands
3. Buttertubs Slough
4. Cluxewe estuary
5. Cowichan estuary
6. Dudley Marsh
7. East Sooke Park
8. Englishman estuary
9. Esquimalt Lagoon
10. Fulford Harbour
11. Island View Beach
12. Lazo Marsh
13. Martindale Flats
14. Mittlenatch Island
15. Nanaimo estuary
16. Nanoose
17. Northumberland Channel
18. Pacific Rim National Park
19. Parksville/Qualicum
20. Puntledge estuary
21. Rosewall Creek
22. Sidney Spit
23. Somenos Lake
24. Swan Lake/Christmas Hill
25. Tsehum Harbour
26. Victoria Harbour

Coastal Birding Sites

Lower Manland/Sunshine Coast

1. **Alaksen:** migratory birds, herons, raptors, songbirds
2. **Boundary Bay:** aquatic birds, raptors
3. **Burnaby Lake:** waterfowl, raptors, songbirds
4. **Chehalis River:** waterfowl, swans, raptors
5. **Christie Islet:** nesting seabirds
6. **Duck, Barbar and Woodward islands:** aquatic birds
7. **Forslund/Watson Property:** forest birds
8. **Harrison River:** waterfowl, herons, eagles
9. **Ladner Marsh:** aquatic birds
10. **McGillivary Creek:** waterfowl
11. **Pitt-Addington Marsh:** aquatic birds, breeding sandhill cranes
12. **Porpoise Bay:** waterfowl, seabirds
13. **Reifel Migratory Bird Sanctuary:** aquatic birds, raptors, songbirds
14. **Roberts Bank:** aquatic birds
15. **Sea/Iona islands:** waterfowl, seabirds, songbirds
16. **Serpentine River:** aquatic birds
17. **Widgeon Valley:** migratory birds

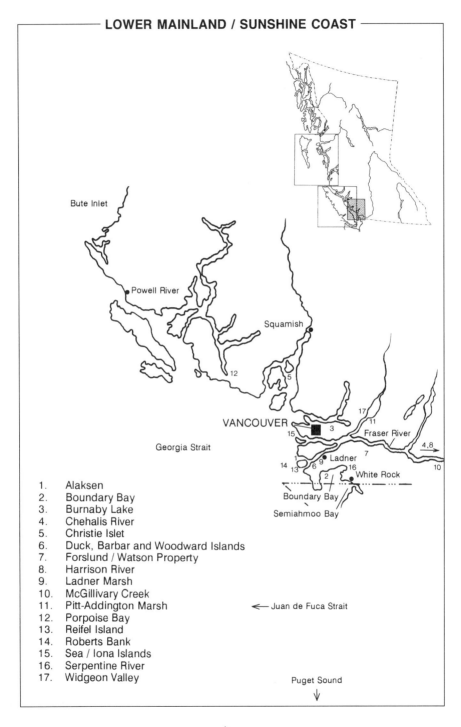

LOWER MAINLAND / SUNSHINE COAST

Bute Inlet

Powell River

Squamish

12

5

VANCOUVER

15   3

17   11

Fraser River

Georgia Strait

4,8

1   7

14   6   9   Ladner   16

13   2   White Rock   10

Boundary Bay

Semiahmoo Bay

1. Alaksen
2. Boundary Bay
3. Burnaby Lake
4. Chehalis River
5. Christie Islet
6. Duck, Barbar and Woodward Islands
7. Forslund / Watson Property
8. Harrison River
9. Ladner Marsh
10. McGillivary Creek
11. Pitt-Addington Marsh
12. Porpoise Bay
13. Reifel Island
14. Roberts Bank
15. Sea / Iona Islands
16. Serpentine River
17. Widgeon Valley

←— Juan de Fuca Strait

Puget Sound
↓

Coastal Birding Sites

Queen Charlotte Islands/North Coast

1. **Delkatla Slough:** aquatic and upland birds, sandhill cranes, trumpeter swans
2. **Lower Skeena River:** shorebirds, raptors
3. **Rose Spit/Naikoon Park:** aquatic birds, raptors
4. **Skedans, Limestone, and Reef islands:** aquatic birds
5. **South Moresby:** seabirds

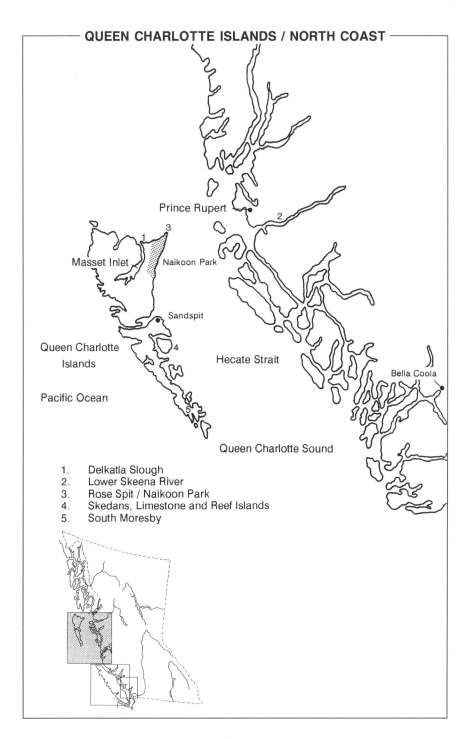

QUEEN CHARLOTTE ISLANDS / NORTH COAST

Prince Rupert

Masset Inlet

Naikoon Park

Sandspit

Queen Charlotte
Islands

Hecate Strait

Bella Coola

Pacific Ocean

Queen Charlotte Sound

1. Delkatla Slough
2. Lower Skeena River
3. Rose Spit / Naikoon Park
4. Skedans, Limestone and Reef Islands
5. South Moresby

Coastal Bird Species

Red-throated loon
Pacific loon
Common loon
Yellow-billed loon

Pied-billed grebe
Horned grebe
Red-necked grebe
Western grebe
Eared grebe

Black-footed albatross
Laysan albatross

Northern fulmar
Pink-footed shearwater
Flesh-footed shearwater
Sooty shearwater
Short-tailed shearwater
New Zealand shearwater
Manx shearwater

Fork-tailed storm-petrel
Leach's storm-petrel
Scaled petrel

Brown pelican

Double-crested cormorant
Brandt's cormorant
Pelagic cormorant
Red-faced cormorant

Magnificent frigatebird

American bittern
Great blue heron
Great egret

Cattle egret
Green-backed heron
Black-crowned night-heron

Tundra swan
Trumpeter swan
Mute swan
Greater white-fronted goose
Canada goose
Snow goose
Emperor goose
Brant
Mallard
Wood duck
Green-winged teal
Blue-winged teal
Cinnamon teal
Northern Pintail
Northern shoveller
Gadwall
Eurasian wigeon
American wigeon
Canvasback
Redhead
Ring-necked duck
Greater scaup
Lesser scaup
Common eider
King eider
Steller's eider
Tufted duck
Harlequin duck
Oldsquaw
Black scoter
Surf scoter
White-winged scoter
Common goldeneye
Barrow's goldeneye

Bufflehead
Hooded merganser
Common merganser
Red-breasted merganser
Ruddy duck

Osprey
Bald eagle
Golden eagle
Northern harrier
Sharp-shinned hawk
Northern goshawk
Red-tailed hawk
Rough-legged hawk
Cooper's hawk
Marsh hawk

American kestrel
Merlin
Peregrine falcon
Gyrfalcon

Turkey vulture

Ring-necked pheasant
Blue grouse
Ruffed grouse
Rock ptarmigan
California quail

Virginia rail
Sora
American coot

Sandhill crane

Black oystercatcher

American avocet

Black-bellied plover

Lesser golden plover
American golden plover
Snowy plover
Semipalmated plover
Killdeer

Greater yellowlegs
Lesser yellowlegs
Wandering tattler
Spotted sandpiper
Upland sandpiper
Solitary sandpiper
Rock sandpiper
Sharp-tailed sandpiper
Pectoral sandpiper
Baird's sandpiper
Least sandpiper
Stilt sandpiper
Semipalmated sandpiper
Western sandpiper
Buff-breasted sandpiper
Curlew sandpiper
Long-billed curlew
Surfbird
Whimbrel
Marbled godwit
Hudsonian godwit
Ruddy turnstone
Black turnstone
Red knot
Sanderling
Dunlin
Ruff
Long-billed dowitcher
Short-billed dowitcher
Common snipe
Red phalarope
Red-necked phalarope
Wilson's phalarope
Northern phalarope

Pomarine jaeger
Parasitic jaeger
Long-tailed jaeger
Skua
South polar skua

Franklin's gull
Bonaparte's gull
Mew gull
Ring-billed gull
California gull
Herring gull
Thayer's gull
Western gull
Glaucous gull
Glaucous-winged gull
Sabine's gull
Heermann's gull

Black-legged kittiwake

Caspian tern
Arctic tern
Common tern
Aleutian tern
Black tern
Forster's tern

Common murre
Thick-billed murre
Pigeon guillemot
Marbled murrelet
Ancient murrelet
Cassin's auklet
Rhinoceros auklet
Tufted puffin
Horned puffin

Rock dove
Mourning dove
Band-tailed pigeon

Great horned owl
Snowy owl
Long-eared owl
Short-eared owl
Northern saw-whet owl
Barn owl
Western screech owl
Northern pygmy owl
Spotted owl
Barred owl

Common nighthawk

Black swift
Vaux's swift

Rufous hummingbird
Anna's hummingbird
Calliope hummingbird

Belted kingfisher

Lewis's woodpecker
Downy woodpecker
Hairy woodpecker
Pileated woodpecker
Three-toed woodpecker
Red-naped sapsucker
Red-breasted sapsucker
Yellow-bellied sapsucker
Northern flicker

Western flycatcher
Olive-sided flycatcher
Willow flycatcher
Hammond's flycatcher
Pacific-slope flycatcher
Ash-throated flycatcher
Say's phoebe
Eastern kingbird
Western kingbird

Tropical kingbird
Western wood pewee

Horned lark

Tree swallow
Violet green swallow
Barn swallow
Cliff swallow
Bank swallow
Rough-winged swallow
Purple martin

Steller's jay
Gray jay
Clark's nutcracker
Northwestern crow
Common raven

Chestnut-backed chickadee
Black-capped chickadee
Mountain chickadee
Bushtit
Red-breasted nuthatch
Brown creeper

American dipper
House wren
Winter wren
Marsh wren
Bewick's wren

Golden-crowned kinglet
Ruby-crowned kinglet
Northern wheatear
Mountain bluebird
Western bluebird

Townsend's solitaire
Swainson's thrush
Hermit thrush

Varied thrush
American robin

Water pipit
Gray catbird

Bohemian waxwing
Cedar waxwing
Northern shrike
European starling
Crested myna
Hutton's vireo
Solitary vireo
Warbling vireo
Red-eyed vireo
Black-throated gray warbler
Orange-crowned warbler
Nashville warbler
Yellow warbler
Yellow-rumped warbler
Townsend's warbler
Palm warbler
MacGillivray's warbler
Wilson's warbler
Common yellowthroat
Northern waterthrush
American redstart
Western tanager
Black-headed grosbeak
Evening grosbeak
Pine grosbeak
Lazuli bunting
Rufous-sided towhee
Vesper sparrow
Lark sparrow
American tree sparrow
Chipping sparrow
Savannah sparrow
Fox sparrow
Lincoln's sparrow
White-throated sparrow

White-crowned sparrow
Harris's sparrow
House sparrow
Tree sparrow
Song sparrow
Swamp sparrow
Golden-crowned sparrow
Dark-eyed junco
Lapland longspur
Smith's longspur
Chestnut-collared longspur
Eurasian skylark
Snow bunting
McKay's bunting
Red-winged blackbird
Brewer's blackbird
Yellow-headed blackbird

Rusty blackbird
Northern oriole
Great-tailed grackle
Brown-headed cowbird
Western meadowlark

Brambling
Purple finch
House finch
American goldfinch
Gray-crowned rosy finch
Red crossbill
White-winged crossbill
Common redpoll
Pine siskin
Dickcissel

Books for Birders

Campbell, Wayne et al. *The Birds of British Columbia, Vols. I and II.* Victoria, B.C.: Royal B.C. Museum, 1990.

Campbell, Wayne and Eileen, and McLaughlin, Ronald T. *Waterbirds of Georgia Strait.* Vancouver, B.C.: British Columbia Waterfowl Society, 1991.

Dunn, Jon L. and Blom, Eirik A. T. *Field Guide to the Birds of North America.* Washington, D.C.: National Geographic Society, (second edition) 1987.

Ehrlich, Paul R.; Dobkin, David S. and Wheye, Darryl. *The Birder's Handbook.* Simon & Schuster, 1988.

Farrand, John Jr. *An Audubon Handbook: Western Birds.* New York, NY: McGraw-Hill Book Co., 1988.

Farrand, John Jr. *The Audubon Society Master Guide to Birding* (three volumes). New York, NY: Alfred A. Knopf, 1983.

Kaufman, Kenn. *Advanced Birding (Peterson Field Guide Series).* Boston, MA: Hougton Mifflin, 1990.

Merilees, Bill. *Attracting Backyard Wildlife.* Vancouver, B.C.: Whitecap Books, 1989.

Obee, Bruce and Fitzharris, Tim. *Coastal Wildlife of British Columbia.* Vancouver, B.C.: Whitecap Books, 1991.

Peterson, Roger Tory. *A Field Guide to Western Birds.* Boston, MA: Houghton Mifflin (third edition), 1990.

Taylor, K. *A Birders Guide to Vancouver Island.* Victoria, B.C.: Top Drawer Infosystems, 1990.

Whitman, Ann H. *Familiar Birds of North America: Western Region (Audubon Society Pocket Guide).* New York, NY: Alfred A. Knopf, 1986.

About the Artist

Doug Penhale's cartoons, wildlife sketches, and paintings are published in books and magazines, and adorn homes and buildings in several countries. He was represented in the Canadian Nature Federation's cross-country wildlife exhibition and received the "best overall" in the 1985 First Annual Victoria International Cartoon Festival. He lives on Salt-spring Island with his wife, Carol, and daughters, Christina and Sarah.

Notes

Notes

Notes

Notes

Notes

Notes

Notes

Notes

Notes

Notes

Notes